Contents

Any words appearing in the text in bold, **like this**, are explained in the Glossary.

Crows are birds. There are 116 **species** (kinds) of crows altogether, including ravens, rooks, jackdaws and magpies. Crows are all quite large birds, as big or bigger than pigeons. They have stout, fairly long beaks and they are all intelligent. This book mostly talks about three of the commonest crows – the carrion crow, the hooded crow and the common (or American) crow.

Carrion, hooded and common crows

Carrion and common crows look very similar. They have black feathers and legs, a heavy black beak and large feet. The hooded crow is similar to carrion and common crows, but has some grey feathers.

Carrion crows are usually about 45 centimetres long from beak to tail and weigh about half a kilogram. When they fly, they flap their strong wings quite slowly.

4

Life

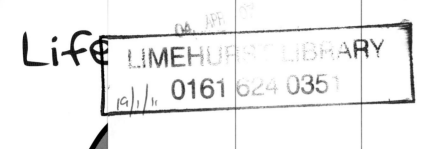

Richard and Louise Spilsbury

Heinemann

A3 067 866 X

www.heinemann.co.uk/library

To order:
☎ Phone 44 (0) 1865 888066
🖹 Send a fax to 44 (0) 1865 314091
🖥 Visit the Heinemann Bookshop at www.heinemann.co.uk/library to browse our
catalogue and order online.

First published in Great Britain by Heinemann Library, Halley Court, Jordan Hill, Oxford OX2 8EJ, part of Harcourt Education.
Heinemann is a registered trademark of Harcourt Education Ltd.

Editorial: Nicole Irving and Georga Godwin
Design: Ron Kamen and Celia Floyd
Picture Research: Catherine Bevan and Kay Altwegg
Production: Lorraine Warner

Originated by Dot Gradations Ltd
Printed in China by Wing King Tong

ISBN 0 431 16925 X (hardback)   ISBN 0 431 16932 2 (paperback)
07 06 05 04 03   08 07 06 05 04
10 9 8 7 6 5 4 3 2 1   10 9 8 7 6 5 4 3 2 1

British Library Cataloguing in Publication Data
Spilsbury, Richard and Spilsbury, Louise
Animal Groups: Crows – Life in a flock
599.8'64'156
A full catalogue record for this book is available from the British Library.

Acknowledgements

The publishers would like to thank the following for permission to reproduce photographs:
Corbis/Tim Zurowski p26; FLPA/D Maslowski p8, /Derek Robinson p24, /GT Andrewartha p22, /John Hawkins p12, /Peggy Heard p20, /R Wilmhurst pp6, 17, /Richard Brooks p13; Gareth Hunt p14; Nature Picture Library/Elio Della Ferrera p21, /Miles Barton p15; NHPA/EA Janes p29, /Helio and Van Ingen p7, /Laurie Campbell p4, /Paal Hermansen p5, /William Paton pp11, 27; Oxford Scientific Films/Carlos Sanchez Alonso p19, /John Geralach/AA p18, /Mike Birkhead p16, /Scott Camazine p23, /St Meyers/OKAPI p10, /Mark Bowler p9.

Cover photograph of rooks in a tree, reproduced with permission of NHPA/EA Janes.

The publishers would like to thank Claire Robinson for her assistance in the preparation of this book.

Every effort has been made to contact copyright holders of any material reproduced in this book. Any omissions will be rectified in subsequent printings if notice is given to the publishers.

What is a bird?

Birds are animals that have wings. Their bodies are covered in feathers and they lay eggs. Birds have **adaptations** (special features) that help them to fly – their bones and feathers are light, but strong, and they have powerful muscles to flap their wings.

Group life

Crows are **social** birds and they spend a lot of their time doing things with other crows, such as sleeping or feeding. A group of crows is often known as a flock, although its proper name is a murder. People in the past probably gave this unpleasant name to crow groups because they sometimes feed on dead animals, and their black colour reminds people of death.

This is a murder, or flock, of crows. Although each crow is an individual and does things by itself, it spends part of its life in a group like this one.

What is a flock of crows like?

Most of the time, crows live in flocks of up to fifteen birds. These flocks are often made up of members from the same family. At the centre of the family are a **male** and a **female** crow, who usually stay together for their whole lives. The other flock members are mostly the sons and daughters of the central pair of crows.

The family is not together all the time. Just like a human family, individual members go off on their own, or in smaller groups. Crows may split up for hours, days or even weeks while they search for food.

A pair of male and female crows spend a lot of time near each other, even helping each other to **preen** (clean and care for) feathers that are difficult to reach.

Know your family

To us, crows may all look similar, but a crow can tell which other crows belong to its flock because it can remember what they look like and what their **calls** sound like.

What is life in a flock like?

In a flock of crows, there is a **pecking order**. This means that some crows are more important than others. The most important crows are the oldest males. These are the **dominant** (leader) birds. Next come the younger males, and then the females. Dominant male crows are usually the ones that start fights with crows from other flocks, and find nest sites or food.

Some young crows stay with their parents for five years or more. When a young male crow finds a female to **breed** with, the new pair often returns to live near his parents. Young females usually leave for good. This is because a female's flock would fight any males from other flocks that she might breed with.

Crows can easily spot other crows, even if they are far away, because their black colour stands out against the daytime sky.

A flock's year

Family flocks tend to remain apart from other crows during the spring and summer months. This is when crows have their young. Families are busy making nests and looking after baby birds. Food is plentiful, so there is enough for crows to eat and to feed their young.

In the cold months of autumn and winter, there is less food about. Crows have to travel further and spend more time looking for their food. At night they gather together with other flocks of crows in **roosts**. A roost is a place where lots of birds rest or sleep, usually on one tree or on several trees close to each other.

Rooks are crows that nest together in big groups of about 50 nests. In some parts of Europe crow cities have been seen with up to 16,000 nests.

What is a roost like?

A crow **roost** is a very noisy place where groups of hundreds or even tens of thousands of crows gather at night. Crows from many different flocks sometimes meet in groups of trees where crows have gathered every winter for years.

Every evening at sunset, the crows appear at the roost, arriving from all directions. After some squabbling and squawking, they all find places to rest and go to sleep. In the morning, they set off again to find food. They usually leave and return by the same route each day.

How do crows sleep?

After settling down in a roost, a crow, like this jackdaw, often **preens**. It then tucks its beak under its feathers and squats down on a branch. It locks its toes and sharp claws around the branch to hold on tightly through the night.

Why come to a roost?

Crows stay in roosts partly to protect themselves from night-time **predators**, such as owls. If a predator attacks a bird, then it or one of its neighbours will produce an alarm **call**. This gives the others a better chance of escaping danger than if they had been sleeping alone.

Many scientists believe that crows also swap information at their roosts. They pass on information in the calls they make, but also in the way they behave. For example, crows may all follow one crow, usually a **dominant** male, which has found a good food source. This is especially important in winter, when food is difficult to find.

Although a roost of crows can be spotted more easily than a smaller group, crows are safer if they stay together.

Where do crows live?

Crows live in lots of different **habitats**, from windswept mountains to city streets. Many crows prefer open spaces and some like high landing places with good views from which to look around. The common, or American, crow is found throughout most of North America. Carrion and hooded crows live in parts of Europe, Asia and the Middle East.

The reason that crows can live in so many different habitats is that they are very adaptable. They can eat almost anything and live almost anywhere. They adapt to changes in their environment by finding new places to live. For example, in areas where woodlands have been cut down to build towns and cities, crows build nests at the top of telegraph poles instead of in trees.

In towns and cities, crows like the carrion crow shown here, use walls as look-out posts to watch for food and enemies.

11

What is a crow's territory?

In the **breeding season**, each pair of crows marks out part of the habitat they live in as their own. This area is called their **territory**. Within the territory the crows can find the food they and their family will need, and a safe place to nest. Territories are bigger in places where there is less food, because the crows have to travel further to get all they need to eat.

Crows **call** from different parts of their territory to tell other crows it is theirs. They chase away any crows from other flocks that come into their territories. These birds are a threat because they might try to take the flock's food, or even eat the flock members' eggs or kill their chicks.

It is not possible for us to see where one crow territory ends and another begins – they do not have fences around them like the fields of neighbouring farms.

What do crows eat?

Crows are **omnivores** – they eat both animals and plants. They are not fussy about whether they eat meat from animals they kill, or **carrion**. In fact, crows eat just about anything they can find or catch – grasshoppers, caterpillars, worms, **grubs**, grain, berries, mice, the eggs and young of other birds and rubbish. If there is not much food nearby, crows will fly for up to 50 kilometres (30 miles) in a day to find enough.

Crows are able to eat so many different foods partly because of their beaks. A crow's beak is strong enough to crack open tough seeds and shells. It is also long and sharp enough to probe about in soil to find and catch wriggling **prey**. After the crow has found food, it uses its strong feet to hold the food while it eats it.

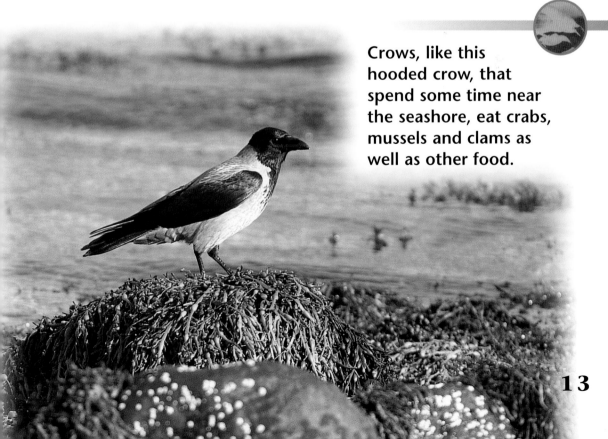

Crows, like this hooded crow, that spend some time near the seashore, eat crabs, mussels and clams as well as other food.

13

Getting the food they want

It is not just because crows eat anything that they are able to live in different **habitats**. They also find ways to make use of what is available to them in ways that many other animals do not. They wash sticky or muddy food before they eat it. They drop shelled animals, such as clams, from great heights to crack the shells so they can eat the animals inside. People have seen hooded crows using their beaks and feet to pull up fishing lines and steal the fish caught on the end.

Using tools ● ● ● ● ● ● ● ● ● ●

Some crows use tools to help them get food. If it hears grubs moving inside branches or beneath leaf litter, a crow may find a twig with a curved end. Using its beak like a knife, the crow removes the bark and leaves and carves the twig into a sharp hook to stick into the leaf litter and catch the grub. New Caledonian crows, like the one in this picture, sometimes carry the tools they have made to other feeding places so they can use them again.

People have seen carrion crows using cars to crack walnuts for them. The crows wait at traffic lights and when the cars stop they fly down and place walnuts on the zebra crossing. After the cars have passed over the nuts and the traffic has stopped again, they swoop down to collect their meal!

Why feed in a flock?

Living in a flock is a good way of getting enough food. If a bird feeds on its own, it has to spend quite a lot of time looking up and checking for danger. If it does not keep watch like this, it may be injured or killed by a **predator**. In a flock, each bird can rely on others to do the checking for some of the time, so it can spend more time feeding.

Crows in this flock take it in turns to feed, while others act as look-outs.

How clever are crows?

When a crow **hatches** out of its egg, it already knows
how to do some things. It knows it must open its beak
and squawk to get food if its parents come to the nest.
It also knows that it should sit quietly in the nest for
the rest of the time, so as not to attract **predators**. The
young crow quickly starts to learn other things, such as
what its family members look like and, eventually, how
to use its wings to fly.

Crows learn quickly.
Young crows learn
how to feed chicks in
the nest by watching
their parents do it.

Crows are particularly clever birds because they learn a
lot by copying other crows in their flock. For example,
if one bird works out a method of opening clams by
dropping them on rocks, other flock members then
learn how to do the same thing by copying.

Learning to avoid danger

One of the most important things crows learn is to recognize and avoid danger. Some crows have learned that a man holding a stick is no threat, while a man holding a gun is to be avoided at all costs. Several members of one flock of ravens learned to avoid a **hide** if hunters were inside.

Amazing memories

One of the reasons crows are so clever is that they have good memories for certain things, such as where food is. They often sit like guards at the top of telegraph poles or trees, watching what is going on. If they see other birds carrying twigs or food to nests, they remember their location. Then they alert other crows so they can all fly back to the nests for a meal of eggs or chicks.

You can't fool a crow!

Cuckoos are birds that lay their eggs in the nests of other birds. When they hatch out, cuckoo chicks throw the other birds' eggs or chicks out of the nest. However, one type of crow, the azure-winged magpie, shown here, has learned that cuckoo eggs look different to their own. These clever magpies throw the cuckoo eggs out of their nests!

Mental maps

Crows seem to carry maps of their **territories** in their heads. One North American crow, the Clark's nutcracker, collects over 30,000 seeds in autumn and buries them in different parts of its territory. This territory can stretch for over 300 square kilometres (115 square miles), but in winter the crow remembers where nine out of every ten seeds are buried!

This Clark's nutcracker lives in Rocky Mountain National Park, USA. These birds have amazing memories – remembering which area they buried seeds in months before.

How do crows communicate?

We **communicate** not just by talking or writing, but also in the way we look and the things we do. Crows use movements that mean something to other crows too, but they communicate mostly using **calls**.

Crows use different calls to mean different things. Most of their 25 calls sound like 'caws' to us, but they are all different. Some are longer or louder than others. These differences change the meaning of the call. For example, one kind of call is used to gather the family together and another is used to sound the alarm when a crow needs help.

Crows make different calls for different **predators**. They make one kind of call if a cat is approaching, and a different kind of call if a hawk is closing in.

Attracting a mate

Male crows, like many other male birds, have a special **display** – a dance or series of movements – that they use to tell a **female** that they want to **breed** with her. If they don't get it right, the female might choose to breed with a different male.

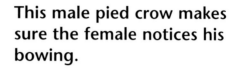
This male pied crow makes sure the female notices his bowing.

First, a male crow spreads his wings and tail and fluffs his feathers up. He bows to the female and struts around, while making a call that sounds a bit like a rattle. He also shows off his flying skills by zooming into the air, diving and turning sharply. If the female is interested, she approaches him and they often **preen** each other.

Copycats

● ● ● ● ● ● ● ● ● ● ● ●

Crows learn how to communicate by copying other crows. Some crows, such as jackdaws, become very good at copying other animals, even learning to imitate cat miaows!

When crows are ready to **breed**, they build a nest. A nest is not usually a bird's home – they build it just to lay their eggs and care for their young.

Baby birds grow inside an egg outside their mother's body. Eggs need to be protected from **predators** and from cold. Parent birds keep eggs warm by covering them with their warm, feathered bodies.

Nest building

A pair of crows makes a new nest together each year in spring, somewhere within their family's **territory**. First they build a rough basket out of sticks and twigs. They then smooth the inside using mud, grass, moss, hair or feathers. This makes the nest softer and less draughty for the eggs, and more comfy for the sitters.

This jackdaw is collecting hair from a horse's back to use in its nest. Crows take around two weeks to collect all the materials they need for their nests.

The early days

Both parents usually take it in turn to keep the eggs warm. Crow chicks **hatch** out of the eggs after about eighteen days. They are blind and have few feathers.

While they are in the nest, the young birds depend on their parents, and sometimes their older brothers and sisters, to bring them food and to remove their droppings. The chicks grow quickly. After a few days, their eyes open and their first feathers emerge. After four or five weeks, all their feathers are fully grown and they have strength enough to fly.

A female common crow lays between three and six bluish, blotchy eggs at a time.

Dunkin' worms ● ● ● ● ● ● ● ● ● ● ● ●

Crow chicks get the water they need from their food. Dry food, such as bread or dried worms, might choke the chicks, so adult crows dunk the food in puddles of water before feeding it to them.

Crows often nest near other crows.
This means that they can spot predators
more quickly, but more predators are also
attracted to the commotion!

Growing up

Most young crows stay with their families for about three years. In this time, their parents usually breed several times, so family flocks can have up to fifteen members. Young crows help by finding nest materials or food for their parents.

After three years, young crows find partners of their own. They nest in or near their parents' territory, especially if the territory contains lots of food. Those who live in territories with little food often move to completely new places, where there may be more food.

Survival

If predators eat their eggs, a pair of crows often has a second lot of chicks. On average, fewer than half the eggs laid survive to become adult crows. Crows can live for up to eight years.

The older brothers and sisters in a flock sometimes act as babysitters, looking after the chicks and bringing them food while the parents are away feeding.

Just like humans, crows argue now and again, and arguments can turn into fights. Fights are more likely when there isn't enough food to go around, and when it is time to **breed**.

Within a family flock, fights are usually short and amount to a few pecks and loosened feathers. **Dominant males** often fight other male family members over who is most important. Sometimes, however, they just **call** and fly acrobatically. This **display** reminds the others how well they might fight if they had to, without risking injuries.

Fighting other crows

Fights with other flocks of crows are different. Crows fly at others they spot on their **territory** and will try to peck and claw them to death. Sometimes they lock claws as they fight, and tumble around in trees and on the ground.

Their speed, strength, sharp beaks and claws make crows good fighters.

Predators

Birds of prey, such as owls and buzzards, are **predators** that eat crows. Animals that climb trees, such as squirrels, racoons and snakes, also try to snatch and eat eggs and crow chicks from their nests. Crows move nest sites each year so predators cannot learn where they are. Some even build a false nest in one place before building their real nest elsewhere.

To defend themselves, crows often get together and **mob** attackers. If a crow sees a predator, it makes an alarm call and any crow from the flock that hears comes to help. Crows sometimes help crows from outside their flock if they are in trouble. By doing a favour for another flock, they might be helped themselves in future.

When crows mob a predator like this eagle, they rarely actually peck it. Instead, they shout at the predator or chase it away.

People problems

Some people dislike crows. They can be a nuisance to farmers because they steal hens' eggs and sometimes damage crops. When they eat **carrion** from dead farm animals, some people think the crows have killed them. When they gather in **roosts** in large numbers, crows are noisy and their droppings are messy. Because of these problems, some people hunt and kill crows.

In many countries there are laws to stop people harming these clever birds. Farmers use other ways to move crows off fields, such as scarecrows and birdscarers (machines that make loud bangs). Near roosts that are becoming a nuisance, people sometimes use recordings of crow warning **calls** to frighten the crows away.

Helpful crows

Crows can actually help farmers to grow crops. They eat the **insects** that would otherwise eat the crops. They can also help clear streets by eating left-over human food and carrion from animals knocked down by cars.

Crow facts

What's the largest crow?

The largest type of crow is the raven, whose body is up to 66 centimetres long – the size of a small vulture. The jackdaw, the smallest crow, is half its size.

Crow sayings

The lookout point on the highest part of a ship is called a 'crow's nest'. This is because crows often build their nests high up in tall trees or on telegraph poles, where they can get a good view of other crows, and also of **predators**.

Crow funeral

Crows sometimes gather in their hundreds around a dead crow. All the crows go quiet, then suddenly fly away together.

Pretty things

Crows, especially magpies, keep a lookout for shiny objects, such as bits of mirror or metal, silver paper and even jewellery. They like to make collections in tree holes or old nests.

Glossary

adaptations special features that allow living things to survive in their particular habitat. For example, polar bears have thick fur to keep them warm in the icy places where they live.

birds of prey birds that hunt and kill other animals for food

breed when animals mate and have babies

breeding season each kind of animal breeds at the same time each year. This is called its breeding season.

call sound, or sequence of sounds, made by an animal

carrion meat eaten from a dead animal that is found dead

communicate pass on a message containing information to another animal or person. Animals communicate in different ways, for example by using calls.

display put on a show of actions that communicates information

dominant leader or most important member of a group of animals

female mature adult animal that can become a mother. A female human is called a woman or girl.

grub young insect without wings, also called a larva

habitat place where an animal or plant lives in the wild

hatch break out of an egg

hide shelter where people go to keep out of sight of animals they want to watch or hunt

insect six-legged small animal with a body divided into three sections – the head, thorax (chest) and abdomen (stomach)

male mature adult animal that can become a father. A male human is called a man or boy.

mob when a group of crows chases away an animal, such as a buzzard

omnivore animal that eats both meat (flesh from other animals) and plants

pecking order order of importance of animals in a group. The highest in the pecking order is the dominant animal, or leader.

predator animal that hunts, catches and eats other animals (the prey)

preen when birds preen, they clean dirt and insects out of their feathers to keep them healthy

prey animal that is hunted and eaten by another animal (the predator)

roost place where birds rest or sleep, usually on the branches of a tree. Large groups of crows gather together in roosts during cold weather.

social living in well-organized groups of animals that work together

species group of living things that are similar in many ways. Male and female animals of the same species can breed to produce healthy young (babies).

territory particular area within a habitat that an animal claims as its own

Books

The Life of Birds, David Attenborough (Collins/BBC, 1998) (also available as a video set)

Carmine the Crow, Heidi Holder (Farrar Straus & Giroux, 1997)

Helm Identification Guides: Crows and Jays, Steve Madge and Hilary Burn (Christopher Helm, 1999)

Websites

More detailed information about the crow family:
   www.shades-of-night.com/aviary/birdfact.html

Simple information about some crow family members:
   www.naturegrid.org.uk/biodiversity/birds/crow.htm#crow

Frequently asked questions about crows:
   birds.cornell.edu/crows/crowfaq.htm

Bird watching and conservation for young people:
   www.rspb.org.uk/youth/

Information about birds in general, based on the BBC TV series *The Life of Birds* by David Attenborough:
   www.pbs.org/lifeofbirds/

Index